W9-CPF-294

Science Made Simple

Grade 1

Written by Vicky Shiotsu
Illustrated by John Carrozza

PHOTO CREDITS
page 50: Elephant photograph by Joe Lange
page 58: Farm photograph by Eric Wunrow
pages 61: Clouds photograph and Icicles photograph by Carlye Calvin
page 76: Birds photograph by Joe Lange

FS-23211 Science Made Simple Grade 1
All rights reserved–Printed in the U.S.A.
Copyright © 1997 Frank Schaffer Publications
23740 Hawthorne Blvd.
Torrance, CA 90505

Introduction

Children have an inherent drive to find out about the world around them. They are curious about what they see or experience, and they often display their interest by asking questions.

How do birds fly?

Do fish breathe?

Why is there a rainbow in the sky?

How come things fall down?

These and other questions are children's attempts to make sense of their environment.

Asking questions is an important part of learning and discovery. *Science Made Simple Grade 1* is designed to help teachers plan a science program that builds upon children's natural inquisitiveness about their world. The numerous hands-on activities in this book encourage children to make observations, ask questions, test ideas, and share results. As you lead the children through the various activities, you can stimulate their thinking by asking thought-provoking questions (suggestions are presented throughout the book) and by allowing the students to branch out into their own investigations. For example, your students may wish to read some of the recommended literature selections or they may want to create new experiments by adapting the ones described in this book.

Science Made Simple Grade 1 can be used alone or as an integral part of any science program. The book is divided into three sections: Life Science, Physical Science, and Earth Science. Each section covers a variety of topics that are interesting, challenging, and age-appropriate. The activities in each section may be introduced sequentially as they appear in the book or in random order.

Science is a subject that encourages exploration, experimentation, and discovery. It is hoped that as you implement the ideas in this book, your students will become better observers, questioners, and problem-solvers. It is also hoped that as your students conduct various investigations, they will enjoy science as a fun, rewarding, and meaningful part of their school experience.

FS-23211 Science Made Simple ▪ © Frank Schaffer Publications, Inc.

Life Science

Children are naturally curious about living things. They are especially fascinated by the insects, worms, lizards, and other creatures they discover directly on their own in their immediate environment. As children study living things and develop an understanding of the characteristics which all living organisms share, they begin to make sense of the way life on Earth is connected; they see that living things—both plants and animals—interact with one another and are dependent on one another for survival.

CONCEPTS

The ideas and activities presented in this section will help children explore the following concepts:

- All living things share certain characteristics.
- Living things need food, water, and air.
- Living things need a place to live.
- Living things grow and change.
- Living things produce other living things of their own kind.

LITERATURE RESOURCES

These colorful, appealing resources will help children learn more about living things.

The Science Book of Things That Grow by Neil Ardley (Harcourt Brace Jovanovich, 1991). The author discusses what is growth, the conditions needed for growth, and many other topics regarding plant life. The book includes simple experiments for children to try.

All Kinds of Animals by Michael Chinery (Random House, 1993). This beautifully illustrated book explains how animals differ from plants, and describes the different groupings of animals.

Flowers by Gallimard Jeunesse, Claude Delafosse and Rene Mettler (Scholastic, 1993) and *The Tree* by Gallimard Jeunesse and Pascale de Bourgoing (Scholastic, 1992). Transparent overlays and brightly colored pictures will fascinate children as they read about different kinds of flowers and trees.

Frog by Angela Royston (Lodestar Books, 1991). This captivating book, part of the See How They Grow series, has simple text and large full-color photos. Other titles include *Duck, Kitten,* and *Puppy.*

Grass and Grasshoppers by Rose Wyler (Julian Messner, 1990). The author shows children how grass differs from other plants in the way it grows, in the type of food it produces, and in its durability. Wyler also invites readers to explore the many kinds of animals that live in the grass.

Living and Nonliving Things

All living organisms have characteristics that distinguish them from nonliving things. For example, living things need nutrients in order to grow and thrive. Most living things have the ability to move and the ability to reproduce their own kind. As you give your class opportunities to compare nonliving things to people, plants, and animals, your students will begin to identify the characteristics that all living things share.

LIVING OR NONLIVING?

Class Activity

Collect these materials ahead of time to use with this activity: a lifelike doll, a houseplant, a plastic plant, pictures of living and nonliving things (one picture for each student in your class).

Call a child to the front of the class. Then hold up the doll beside him or her. Ask the class to brainstorm ways in which the two are alike and different. (Examples: Both have bodies that look alike; one can move on his own but the other cannot.)

Ask the class, *Which one is living—the doll or the student? Why?* Jot your students' ideas on the blackboard. (The children's responses will vary depending on their abilities and experiences. One child may simply state an observation—*The doll is not alive because it cannot move by itself.* Another child may make a statement based on what he or she knows about human beings—*The student is alive because he breathes and needs to have food.*) Guide your students into seeing that their descriptions of their classmate describe most living things.

Next show your class the houseplant and the plastic plant. Ask which of the two is alive and why. Then have the students suggest ways in which their classmate and the living plant are similar. (Examples: They both need food; they both grow and change; they both have "parents.") Tell the class that all living things share these characteristics.

For a follow-up activity, hand out pictures of living and nonliving things to the class. Post a sheet of chart paper in the classroom. Divide the paper into two columns; label one column *Living Things* and the other *Nonliving Things.* Then have each student glue his or her picture onto the correct column.

Art Project

Colorful Collages

Remind your students that the world is made up of living things and nonliving things. Then divide your class into small groups and give each group a large sheet of butcher paper. Assign half the class to make collages of living things and the other half to make collages of nonliving items. Provide newspapers and magazines for the children so that they can cut out pictures for gluing onto their papers. Afterwards, let the students share their work with the class.

PLANTS AND ANIMALS

On the chalkboard ledge, display various pictures of plants, animals, and people. Ask the class what the pictures have in common. (They are pictures of living things.) Review with the class some of the characteristics all living things share. (They need food; they grow; they can usually make other living things of their own kind.)

Next hold up a picture of a plant and a picture of an animal. Ask how the two differ. Accept all reasonable answers from your class. (Examples: *The plant cannot move on its own. The animal uses a mouth to eat food.*) Tell the students that most living things can be classified into two large groups—plants and animals. Ask the students in which group they think people belong. Explain that people are grouped with animals because the two share many common traits such as the ability to move and the need for finding food. Then have the class help you sort the pictures on the chalkboard ledge into plants and animals.

LIVING THINGS LOTTO

Matching Game

Let your students practice classifying plants and animals with this fun lotto game. First divide the class into pairs and give each pair a copy of two lotto boards (page 4) and one set of game cards (page 5). Tell the students to color the lotto boards and game cards and to cut them out. Then have the class make the game cards sturdy by gluing them onto two-inch tagboard squares.

Next give each pair these instructions for playing the game:

1. Scatter the cards facedown on a table or on the floor.

2. Take turns picking up a card and placing it on a matching plant or animal space on the lotto board. If there is no matching space on the lotto board, return the card facedown.

3. The first player to cover all the spaces on his lotto board wins.

Afterwards, have each pair put the game cards and lotto boards in a self-locking plastic freezer bag for easy storage.

Art Project

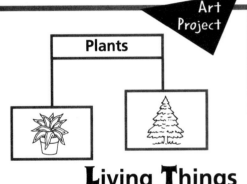

Living Things Mobile

Give each student a copy of the game cards (page 5) and let the class make mobiles of living things. First, have the students color the pictures and cut them out. Next give each student two strips of 2" x 12" tagboard and 20 varying lengths of yarn. Have the students tape yarn to the back of each picture. Then tell the children to label one tagboard strip *Plants* and the other *Animals*, and have them tape the corresponding pictures onto each one.

Living Things Lotto

Animal	Plant	Animal
Plant	Animal	Plant
Animal	Plant	Animal

FS-23211 Science Made Simple ▪ © Frank Schaffer Publications, Inc.

Game Cards

Teacher: See page 3 for suggestions on using these cards.

Basic Needs

All living things need food, water, air, and a place to live. Most plants have the ability to make their own food. Animals, on the other hand, get food by eating plants or other animals. Both plants and animals live in environments that provide the resources necessary for survival.

ALL KINDS OF FOOD

Bring to school a grocery bag filled with various foods. Include foods from plants (such as a potato or a box of rice) and foods from animals (such as an egg or some butter). Also bring samples of foods for pets, such as a can of dog food or a package of bird seed. Take out the items from the bag and ask the class what they have in common. (They are all food.) Tell the students that all living things need food to live and grow. (If the class asks how a plant gets food or wonders about the type of food it needs, tell the students they will be working with plants to find the answers to those questions. See the activities described on page 7.)

Next give a paper plate to each student and have the children glue on magazine pictures to show some of the foods they enjoy. Later, let the students share their work with the class.

SOURCES OF FOOD

Get your grocery bag of foods (see above) and show the items to the class again. Point out that people are able to eat a wide variety of foods. Explain that some of our foods come from animals and some come from plants. Then hold up the various food items and have the class identify their sources.

Next divide the class into pairs and give each pair two large sheets of drawing paper. On one sheet have the students draw or glue on pictures of foods that come from animals; on the other sheet, have them display pictures of foods that come from plants. Instruct the class to label each food item. Afterwards, have the students compare their work with one another.

PET TALK

Invite students who have pets to talk about the food needs of their animals. If possible, let the children bring their pets one at a time to the classroom. Have each pet owner discuss the type of food his or her animal eats, the amount of food and water consumed in a day, and the number of times the animal must be fed daily. Let the class keep track of the information on chart paper.

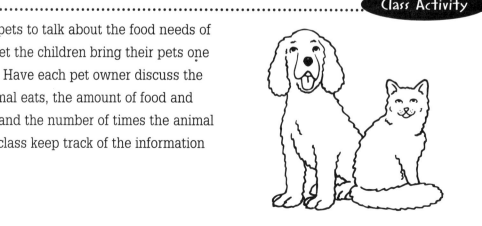

FS-23211 Science Made Simple • © Frank Schaffer Publications, Inc.

FOOD MAKERS

Tell your class that unlike animals that have to find food, most plants are able to make their own food. Then show a potted plant and ask what part of the plant might make food. After the students share their ideas, explain that plants use their leaves to make food. Tell the children they will be doing some experiments to find out what special things plants need in order to enable the leaves to make food.

DO PLANTS NEED WATER?

You will need two potted plants and a small watering can for this experiment. Do this activity as a teacher demonstration or provide enough plants for small groups of children to work with.

Hand out copies of the experiment and record sheets (pages 8 and 9) to the children. Then set the plants in a sunny spot in the classroom. Ask a child to water only one plant. Use masking tape to label the plants *Watered* and *Not Watered*.

Every few days have the class water the plant marked *Watered* just enough to keep the soil moist. After a week, the watered plant will look healthy, but the leaves of the unwatered plant will have turned yellow or brown. Explain that without water, the plant cannot make food and dies.

DO PLANTS NEED SUNLIGHT?

Show the class a potted geranium plant. Cover one leaf completely with aluminum foil. Tell the class that covering the leaf prevents it from getting any sunlight. Then ask the students to predict what will happen to the leaf and write their ideas on a sheet of chart paper. After a week, take the foil off the leaf and let the class examine it. (The leaf will have turned yellow.)

Tell the class that plants need sunlight. The green color of a leaf shows that it has a green chemical (chlorophyll) that is necessary for making the plant's food (sugars). Without sunlight, a plant cannot make this green chemical and the plant will eventually die because it cannot produce food for growth.

DO PLANTS NEED AIR?

Do this activity as a teacher demonstration or a small group activity. First, soak several beans in water overnight. Drain the beans and rinse them. Next line the bottom of two bowls with three sheets of paper towels. Put half the beans in one bowl and cover them completely with water. Put the other half in the second bowl, and add only enough water to moisten the paper towels. Have the students predict what will happen to the beans, and write their ideas on chart paper. The beans in both bowls begin growing, but the seeds that are immersed in water stop growing after a few days. Explain that these seeds did not have enough air to produce food for continued growth.

Do Plants Need Water?

Question:

Do plants need water?

Materials:

two potted plants
small watering can

Directions:

1. Set the plants in a sunny spot.

2. Water one plant every few days. Do not water the other plant. Wait one week.

Prediction:

Get your record sheet.
Write what you think will happen.

Results:

Draw a picture of the plants after a week.
Write about your picture.

Conclusion:

Do plants need water? Write your answer on the record sheet.

FS-23211 Science Made Simple ▪ © Frank Schaffer Publications, Inc.

Do Plants Need Water?

Question:

Do plants need water?

Prediction:

What do you think will happen to the plants?

_____

_____

Results:

Draw a picture to show what the plants looked like after a week. Write about your picture.

_____

_____

_____

_____

Conclusion:

Does a plant need water?

_____

A VERY HUNGRY ANIMAL

Read Eric Carle's *The Very Hungry Caterpillar* (Philomel, 1987) to the class. Discuss with the students all the different things the caterpillar ate during the week. Then let the children have fun writing their own stories about other hungry animals. If you wish, have the students write their stories based on the sentence pattern in Carle's book:

On Monday, the (animal) ate one _____.

On Tuesday, the (animal) ate two _____.

On Wednesday, the (animal) ate three _____.

SEED SURVEY

1-Sunflower Seeds
2-Small yellow Seeds

Here's a fun way for children to observe whether or not birds prefer certain kinds of seeds more than others. First, get a package of bird seed and have the children help you sort the seeds. Place the different groupings in the cups of an egg carton or in individual shallow box lids. Fill the cups or lids so that there are equal amounts of each type of seed. Keep track of the different groups by labeling each cup or lid with a number and then writing the numbers and the descriptions of the seeds on a sheet of paper.

Set the seeds outside in a place that the birds can get to easily. Then let the students check the seeds once a day. (Instruct the class to check the seeds quickly and quietly; if any birds are feeding, the children should not approach them.) After a week, have the children evaluate the seeds to see if some kinds were eaten more than others.

COUNTING BREATHS

Ask your class why people cannot live underwater. When a child suggests that people need air, tell the class that all land animals must breathe air to live. (Land animals take in oxygen from the air. Fish and other sea creatures take in oxygen, too, but they get it from the water.)

Next ask the students if they think all people breathe at the same rate. To check their ideas, time the students for one minute while they breathe normally and count their breaths. (One inhale and exhale count as one breath.) Then write on the chalkboard the number of breaths each student took and have the class compare the results.

Growth and Change

As living things mature, they grow, develop, and change. In some cases, the young looks similar to the adult; a human baby, for example, looks like a smaller version of an adult human. In other cases, the difference in appearance is quite dramatic, such as in the change a caterpillar undergoes when it becomes a butterfly. Living things do not grow at the same rate nor to the same extent. A tiny redwood seed grows into a tree that is over 300 feet tall; other kinds of seeds grow into much smaller plants. A baby guinea pig grows until it is five times its weight as an adult; a baby elephant, however, will have gained 60 times its weight when it reaches adulthood.

LOOK HOW I'VE GROWN!

Class Activity

Remind your class that all living things share the characteristic of growth. Tell your students that they will be finding out how much they have grown since they were born. Then as a homework assignment, ask the students to find out how long they were at birth. When all the children have gotten their answers, try this activity with them.

Have each child write the length he or she was at birth on a sheet of chart paper. Then secure a measuring tape to a wall. Divide the class into pairs, instruct the children to take off their shoes, and have the partners measure each other's heights. Have the children add their heights to the chart paper.

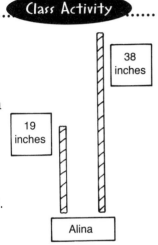

38 inches

19 inches

Alina

Next instruct each child to cut a length of string to show how long they were at birth and another length to show how tall they are now. Let each child tape his or her strings to a long sheet of butcher paper, labeling the length of each and writing his or her name beside the strings. Display the papers in the hallway. Your students will be amazed at how much each of them has grown in a few years.

LONGER BABIES, TALLER CHILDREN?

Class Activity

Use your students' findings about their current heights and their lengths at birth to do this extension activity. First ask the class, *Do you think the tallest children in the class are the ones who were the longest at birth?* After the students answer, ask for suggestions on how they might find out the answer. Accept all reasonable responses, and have the children test their ideas. Here is one suggestion:

Take the current heights from the chart (see *Look How I've Grown!* activity) and rewrite them horizontally on another sheet of paper. Order the heights from the shortest to the tallest, and include the names of the students above their heights. Then under each student's name and height, write the length at birth. Have the children look to see if the longest lengths correspond to the tallest children. (Because children's growth rates vary, your results may vary, but generally, longer babies grow into taller children.)

WHO'S THE BABY?

Discuss how your students' appearances have changed from when they were first born. Then ask the children to bring baby photos of themselves to share with the class. Each day post five or six pictures on a bulletin board and number them. Have the class look at the photos and try to identify the babies. Let each child write his guesses on a sheet of paper. At the end of the day, go over the answers with the children. Ask them what clues they looked for when they were making their guesses. Also ask if some babies were easier to recognize than others and why.

For a fun variation, ask members of your school staff to bring baby photos of themselves. Don't forget to include your picture with theirs. Add the photos to your bulletin board display. Your students will enjoy finding out how the school staff members looked when they were young!

WHAT WILL I LOOK LIKE?

Bring photos of yourself as a young child, a teenager, and an adult, and show them to your class.

If you can, also bring photos of other people at various stages in their lives. Show the pictures to your students. Ask such questions as, *Can you tell that the child and the teenager are the same person? What things have changed as the person got older? What things have stayed the same?* Discuss the fact that even though a person's face changes with age, he or she can often be recognized. Talk about what makes up a person's "looks"—the overall shape of the face; the size and position of the eyes, nose, and mouth; facial expressions that include a characteristic smile or a crinkling of the nose. Tell the class that these factors often remain with a person throughout his or her life.

Next have the children imagine what they will look like in five years. Ask these questions to guide their thinking: *How old will you be? What will your hair look like? How tall will you be? Will you look like one of your brothers or sisters? Will you look like one of your parents? What things about you will be the same as they are now? What things will be different?* Then have each student draw a picture showing how he or she might look in five years.

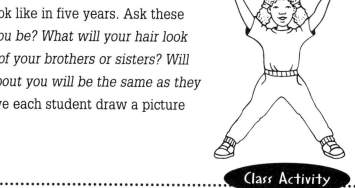

I'M GROWING UP

Tell your students that as babies grow, their bodies change, they learn new things, and they acquire many skills. Then brainstorm with the students the various ways they differ from when they were babies. Write their ideas on a sheet of chart paper. On the left side of the paper write phrases describing the children as babies; on the right side, write descriptions of the children as they are now. (Examples: *Babies—cannot walk, are too small to sleep in a bed, need help eating, need help dressing, cannot eat many kinds of food. Children—can walk by themselves, can eat by themselves, know how to read*) Then give each student a copy of *I'm Growing Up* (page 13) and have the children complete the sentences with words or phrases. (Examples: *I could not reach the sink . . . I did not know how to tie my shoes . . . I needed help dressing myself.*)

I'm Growing Up

Write about when you were a baby.

Write about how you are now.

Look at how you are growing up!

When I was a baby, I could not

_____
- -
_____

But now I can!

When I was baby, I did not know how to

_____
- -
_____

But now I do!

When I was a baby, I needed help

_____
- -
_____

But now I can do that all by myself!

ANIMALS GROW AND CHANGE

Show your class pictures of different baby animals. Tell the class that all baby animals grow and change, but that there is variety in how much they change. Explain that some baby animals, like the giraffe and the sea turtle, are born looking a lot like the adult animals. Others look quite different from their adult version. A black monkey called the langur, for example, gives birth to a bright orange baby. Add that some baby animals, like the caterpillar and the tadpole, change so greatly that the baby and the adult look very different from each other.

Next have your students find out how various animals look as babies and as adults. Divide the class into pairs and have each pair choose an animal to research. Let the students look up their animals in library books and animal magazines, and have each pair draw their animal as a baby and as an adult. Later, display the pictures and have the class separate them into three categories: *Animals That Change a Little*, *Animals That Change Quite a Lot*, and *Animals That Change Greatly*.

LIFE OF A BUTTERFLY

Show your students a picture of a caterpillar and a butterfly, and have them identify the animals. Ask your class how the two are related. (The caterpillar becomes a butterfly.) Tell your class that the caterpillar undergoes a great change (called metamorphosis) when it becomes an adult.

Next give your class a copy of *Life of a Butterfly* (page 15), and have the students color the pictures and cut out the wheels. Give each child a brad fastener for securing the wheels together. As your students turn their wheels, discuss each stage of the butterfly's life cycle. Here are some facts you may want to share:

Egg – Most butterfly eggs are laid on plants. Many eggs are laid at one time. (Depending on the type of butterfly, the number of eggs varies from several dozen to hundreds.) Some eggs hatch in a few days; others take several months.

Larva – The larva (caterpillar) hatches from the egg and begins eating. Often it eats its own eggshell first and then eats the plant on which it hatched. As the caterpillar grows, it sheds its old skin and forms a new one. The caterpillar gets a new skin four or five times.

Pupa – After about two weeks, the caterpillar reaches its full size, sheds its final skin, and changes into a pupa. The pupa is covered with a hard shell and hangs from a twig. Inside the shell the pupa forms into a butterfly.

Adult – The adult butterfly comes out of the shell. Most butterflies live only a week or two, but some kinds live for up to 18 months.

FS-23211 Science Made Simple ■ © Frank Schaffer Publications, Inc.

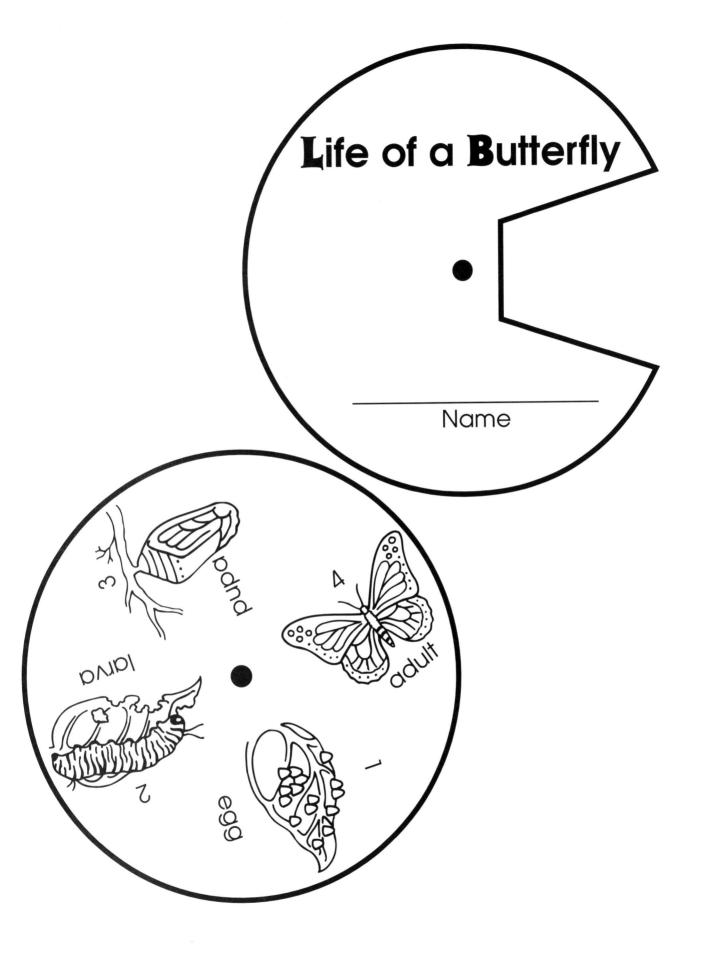

LIFE OF A FROG

Show your class some pictures of frogs. Tell the students that frogs, like butterflies, go through many changes as they grow into adults. Then let the class browse through various library books that show pictures of the frog in various stages of its life. Discuss these stages with your class:

Egg – Most frog eggs are laid in the water. Some frogs lay thousands of eggs at one time!

Tadpole – The baby frog (tadpole) hatches from its egg looking like a little fish. It has a long tail and breathes from gills. As the tadpole gets bigger, it grows a pair of back legs. Then its lungs and front legs begin developing, and its tail gets shorter and shorter. Just before it becomes an adult, the frog loses its gills.

Adult – The tail disappears and the frog becomes an adult. It usually takes a few months for the frog to change from a newly hatched tadpole to an adult.

For a follow-up activity, give each student a copy of *Life of a Frog* (page 17). Have the students color the pictures, cut out the pages, and staple them together to make a minibook they can share at home.

Growing, Playing, Learning

Tell your class that some animals have fun "playing" with each other, much like children do. Add that sometimes playtime actually is a time of learning important skills. For example, lion cubs develop stalking and hunting skills as they have fun pouncing on their mother's moving tail.

Next let your class look at library books, animal magazines, and other resources for information about young animals at play. Two colorful, easy-to-read resources are *Snow Babies* by Eric Rosser (Owl Magazine/Golden Press, 1985) and *A Time for Playing* by Ron Hirschi (Cobblehill Books, 1994). Afterwards, instruct each student to make a picture of a young animal at play and have him or her write a sentence about the picture. Bind the pictures together, add a cover titled *Animals Grow, Play, and Learn*, and display the booklet in your classroom library.

FS-23211 Science Made Simple ■ © Frank Schaffer Publications, Inc.

Life of a Frog

Name _____

1

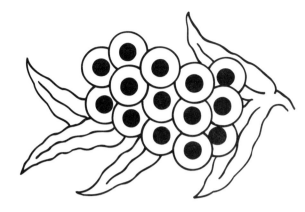

The mother frog lays eggs.

2

A tadpole hatches.

3

The tadpole grows back legs.

4

The tadpole grows front legs.

5

The tadpole becomes an adult.

WATCH A SEED GROW

Your students will be fascinated as they watch a bean transform from a seed into a plant right before their eyes!

This activity may be done individually, in pairs, or in small groups. First, prepare the beans by soaking them in water overnight. Then give the students the experiment card (page 19) and guide them through the instructions.

Have the children observe their beans for two weeks. (Make sure they add enough water every day to the jar to keep the paper towels moist.) Make five copies of the record sheet (page 20) for each child, and have the students make a picture to show what their bean looks like each day. Here are some things that your class can look for as the beans grow and develop:

A tiny root pushes through the bean's outer skin.

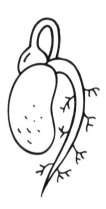

The root grows downward. A shoot starts to grow up out of the bean.

The shoot becomes a leafy stem. Tiny roots have grown from the main root.

BOOKS ABOUT SEEDS

There are a variety of colorful picture books that tell the story of how a seed grows and changes. Here are three your students will enjoy:

The Tiny Seed by Eric Carle (Picture Book Studio, 1987). The author tells the story of how one tiny seed travels all over the world until it settles into fertile ground and grows into a beautiful flower.

From Seed to Plant by Gail Gibbons (Holiday House, 1991). Easy-to-understand text and bright, bold pictures help explain how seeds form, travel, and grow.

I'm a Seed by Jean Marzollo (Scholastic, 1996). A marigold seed and a pumpkin seed grows up side by side. The story is told through "conversations" between the two seeds. The simple text and attractive paper collages invite children to look at the book again and again.

FS-23211 Science Made Simple ■ © Frank Schaffer Publications, Inc.

Watch a Seed Grow

Question:

What happens when a seed grows?

Materials:

tall glass jar
bean
two paper towels
bowl of water

Directions:

1. Soak the bean in water overnight.

2. Roll up the paper towels. Put them in the jar.
   They should touch the sides of the jar.

3. Put the bean between the paper towels
   and the jar.

4. Add water to wet the paper towels.
   Set the jar in a warm place.

5. Watch your bean for two weeks.
   Add enough water every day to keep
   the paper towels moist.

Results:

Draw a picture of your plant every day.

FS-23211 Science Made Simple ▪ © Frank Schaffer Publications, Inc.

Watch a Seed Grow

Date

Date

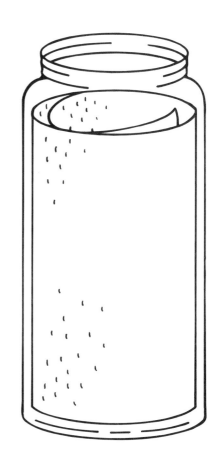

FS-23211 Science Made Simple ▪ © Frank Schaffer Publications, Inc.

New Living Things

Nearly all living things have the ability to reproduce—to create new living things of their own kind. (Some hybrids, such as mules, are not able to reproduce.) Animals produce babies that grow to adulthood. Plants make seeds that grow into new plants. A species that stopped reproducing would become extinct. Reproduction ensures the continuation of living things from one generation to the next.

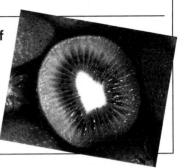

BABIES AND PARENTS

Share some books that show pictures of baby animals and their parents. An ideal book for reading aloud is Masayuki Yabuuchi's *Whose Baby?* (Philomel, 1985) or Deborah Guarino's *Is Your Mama a Llama?* (Scholastic, 1989). The colorful pictures, simple text, and riddlelike format will delight young readers.

As your students look at the pictures, ask *Can a mother and father duck have a baby bear? Can a mother deer give birth to a baby cat?* Guide the class into concluding that parents have babies that are just like them.

Next give the students copies of *Animal Babies* (page 22) and *Animal Parents* (page 23). Have the children cut out the cards and glue them to three-inch squares of tagboard. Then have the children see if they can pair up the babies with their parents. Discuss how some babies look very similar to their parents while others (such as the tadpole) look very different. Then have the children put their cards in plastic resealable bags for easy storage. The cards may be used for other activities. (See below.)

USING THE ANIMAL CARDS

Memory Match—Pair up the students. Each pair plays with one set of cards. The students lay the cards facedown. Each player takes a turn choosing two cards and turning them over. If he has chosen a baby and its parent, he keeps the cards. If the cards do not match, he returns them facedown. The game continues until all the cards have been matched. The player with the most cards wins.

Animal Cover-up—Two or three players may play. Each player gets a sheet of paper with a 2" x 3" grid and on it writes the names of three baby animals and their parents (seal/seal pup; polar bear/polar bear cub; owl/owlet; frog/tadpole; eagle/eaglet; lion/lion cub; fox/fox pup; deer/fawn; duck/duckling). The players then place the cards in a brown paper bag and take turns drawing a card. If a player picks a card that matches a name on his paper, he places it on the corresponding space. If the card does not match, he returns it. The first player to cover his paper wins.

Animal Scramble—Give half your class the parent cards and half the class the corresponding baby cards. Then see how long it takes for the parents and babies to find each other. (Join in the game if you have an odd number of children.) For an extra challenge, set a time limit for the game.

Animal Babies

duckling

fox pup

owlet

eaglet

tadpole

lion cub

seal pup

fawn

polar bear cub

FS-23211 Science Made Simple ▪ © Frank Schaffer Publications, Inc.

Animal Parents

seal

polar bear

owl

frog

eagle

lion

fox

deer

duck

WHO'S HATCHING?

Show pictures of animals with their babies. Tell the class that nearly all living things have the ability to make new living things. Explain that animals can make new animals and plants can make new plants. Add that both animals and plants produce living things that grow up to be like them.

Next show pictures of animals that hatch from eggs, such as a chicken, a snake, and an alligator. Ask what the animals have in common. Guide the class into seeing that some animals have young that hatch from eggs. Then brainstorm with the students a list of animals that lay eggs, and write their suggestions on the chalkboard. You may wish to share books such as Robert Burton's *Egg* (Dorling Kindersley, 1994) or Gallimard Jeunesse and Pascale de Bourgoing's *The Egg* (Scholastic, 1992) for this activity.

Later give the students copies of *Who's Hatching?* (page 25) and these instructions:

1. Choose an animal that hatches from an egg and draw it on the blank egg. Make the picture above the jagged line. Write the animal's name beside its picture.

2. Write one or more clues about the animal on the second egg.

3. Cut out the eggs and staple the smaller egg on top of the larger one. Write your name on the back.

Afterwards, let the children read their clues while the rest of the class guesses the animals.

FAMILIES GROW AND GROW

This activity lets children see that people's families grow and expand with each generation.

First, ask the students to think about the people in their families. Then ask a volunteer to name his or her family members while you list the names on the chalkboard. Include grandparents, aunts, uncles, and cousins. Ask the class *How did this family get to be so big?* Help the students see that as people grow up, marry, and have children, their immediate and extended families grow. Tell the class that families can continue growing this way for many, many years.

For homework, give each student a copy of *My Family* (page 26). Have children ask their parents to help them write down the names of their family members. Then have each child tally the number of people listed. After the students bring their completed papers to school, let them compare the sizes of the families. Ask questions such as *Who has the largest number of people in the immediate family? How many students have more than five cousins? How many in the classroom are an only child? Who has the most people listed on the page?* Ask the students how the information on their papers would change if they grew up, married, and had children. (They would need to add more names to their lists.)

Who's Hatching?

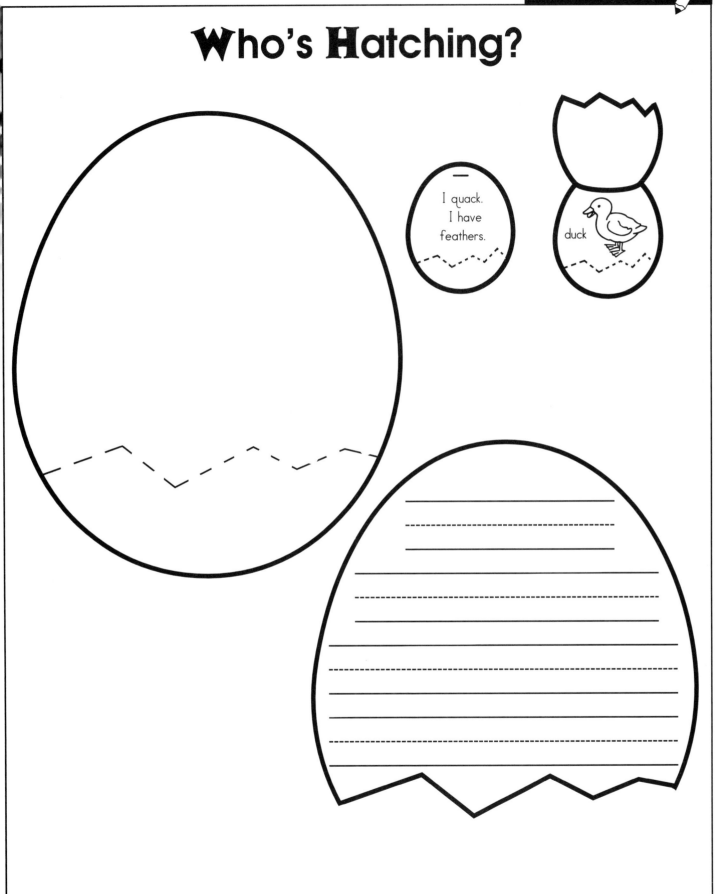

I quack.
I have
feathers.

duck

My Family

Your family includes many people. Write their names below.

Immediate family

(parents, yourself, brothers, sisters)

Grandparents

Aunts, Uncles, Cousins

How many people did you list? _____

FS-23211 Science Made Simple ▪ © Frank Schaffer Publications, Inc.

Physical Science

Young children learn about the world by interacting with their surroundings. They stack blocks and watch them fall; they push toy cars in order to send them moving forward; they bang objects together, enjoying the sound that is produced. As children explore their environment and examine and manipulate objects, they make discoveries about how things work. These discoveries lead to a greater understanding of the forces and principles that govern the physical world.

CONCEPTS

The ideas and activities presented in this section will help children explore the following concepts:

- *Force is needed to move things.*

- *There are different kinds of movements.*

- *Machines help people move things more easily.*

- *There are different kinds of simple machines.*

- *Sound is produced when an object vibrates (moves back and forth).*

- *Sounds can vary.*

LITERATURE RESOURCES

These colorful resources will help children learn more about the physical world.

The Science Book of Motion by Neil Ardley (Harcourt Brace Jovanovich, 1992). Children will enjoy various experiments, including testing how different objects slide and seeing how rollers move loads.

The Science Book of Sound by Neil Ardley (Harcourt Brace Jovanovich, 1991). Students can try several fun experiments, such as making a simple telephone and creating a "pipe-bottle organ."

Amusement Park Machines by Christine Hahn (Raintree, 1979). This book presents machines used in amusement parks, such as the roller coaster and ferris wheel. The author points out the different kinds of movements (spin, swing, slide, float), speeds, and heights visitors can experience at these parks.

Force and Movement by Barbara Taylor (Franklin Watts, 1990). Children learn about how force affects movement. The simple text, full-color photos, and step-by-step experiments will appeal to students.

Sound by Angela Webb (Franklin Watts, 1988). This simple resource helps young children become aware of how sound is produced, how sound travels, and how sounds vary.

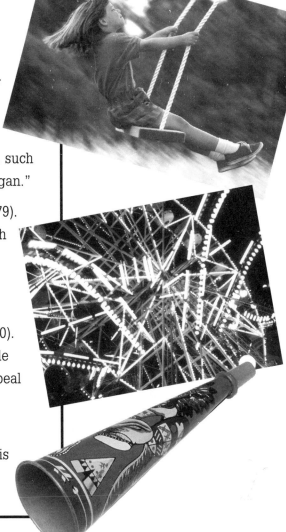

Moving Things

The whole world is in motion. People walking, birds flying, leaves falling, wheels turning—all of these actions involve movement. Movement occurs when an object changes place. Force—the act of a push or a pull—is needed to make something move. In people and animals, the force is exerted by muscles; in inanimate objects, the force is produced by some outside source.

THINGS MOVE AROUND US

Class Activity

Write these words on the chalkboard: *walk, run, spin, roll, jump*. Read the list and ask the class what the words have in common. (They all describe a way of moving.) Tell the students that all around them things are moving, and have the class name a few examples (cars moving along the road, bugs crawling in the grass, children playing in the yard, and so on). Then let the class go outside for several minutes and observe things in motion. When the students return to the classroom, have them compile a list of the things they saw moving.

WHAT MOVED? **Class Activity**

This fun observation game helps your class identify things that have moved. Begin by asking the students what movement is or how they know something has moved. Talk about the fact that when something moves, it changes place. Then stand 10 different books against the chalkboard ledge. Next instruct the students to close their eyes while you switch the positions of two books. Have the children open their eyes and tell you which books have changed places. Continue the game with a child moving the next pair of books.

For a follow-up activity, divide the class into pairs and give each pair a copy of *What Moved?* (page 29). Instruct the students to cut out the toys at the bottom of the page and place them on the shelves. Have one partner close his or her eyes while the other switches the positions of two toys. The first partner guesses which toys have moved. The students then reverse roles.

Art Project

Many Things Move

Remind the class that many different things move. Then instruct the students to cut out magazine pictures of things in motion and glue them onto a large sheet of butcher paper. Have the children include both living and nonliving things on their collage. (Examples: birds soaring, kites flying) Afterwards, have the children identify the various things in motion. Discuss the fact that both living and nonliving things can move or be moved. Guide the class into seeing that most living things can move on their own while nonliving things need something else to move them. (Examples: Birds can fly of their own power while kites need people or wind to move them.)

What Moved?

MAKING THINGS MOVE

Class Activity

Place a small ball on a table so that it does not move. Then ask the students what they could do to make the ball move along the table. (Examples: push the ball so that it starts rolling; blow on the ball, pick up the ball and bounce it across) Have the children demonstrate their ideas for moving the ball.

Next put a cup on the table and ask the children to demonstrate different ways of moving it. (Examples: push, lift, or pull the cup)

Discuss with the class what happened. Tell the students that the ball and the cup could not move by themselves; a force, such as a push or a pull, was needed to make them move. Explain that people cannot see forces, but they can see their effects.

I CAN MOVE LOTS OF THINGS! Class Activity

Show pictures of people moving things, such as a person carrying groceries, a child moving a toy along the floor, a person mowing the lawn, and a cook mixing batter in a bowl. Have the class identify the different things that are being moved in the pictures. Next ask the students to name different things they have moved (pushed, pulled, or lifted) that day. Make a list of their responses on chart paper. Label the paper "I Can Move Lots of Things!"

Afterwards, discuss with the students the various parts of the body that help them move things. (Examples: hands, arms, legs, back) Ask how each of these body parts works to move things. (Examples: hands grab; arms push, pull, or lift; legs walk; back bends) Tell the class that people and animals have muscles that make their body parts move, allowing them to perform such actions as pushing, pulling, and lifting.

MOVING LIGHT AND HEAVY OBJECTS

Group Experiment

Ask the class which would require more force—moving heavy or light objects. Then let the students try this experiment to test their guesses.

First divide the class into pairs and give each pair a copy of *Moving Light and Heavy Objects* (pages 31 and 32). Each pair needs a toy truck, two books that will fit on the truck, some tape, and a rubber band for the experiment. Before the children try the activity, let them pull their rubber bands. Have them notice that the harder they pull—that is, the more force they exert—the longer the rubber band becomes. After the class does the experiment, discuss the fact that heavier objects need more force than lighter objects to be moved.

FS-23211 Science Made Simple ▪ © Frank Schaffer Publications, Inc.

Moving Light and Heavy Objects

Question:

The push or pull needed to move an object is called force. Which takes more force—moving a light object or a heavy object?

Prediction:

Write what you think on the record sheet.

Materials:

toy truck
two books
tape
rubber band

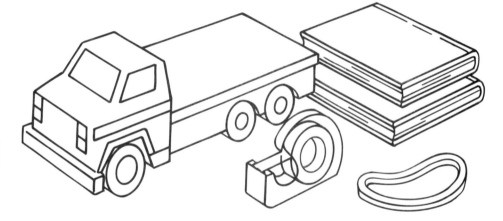

Directions:

1. Tape the rubber band to the front of the truck.

2. Put a book on the truck. Pull the truck. Look at how long the rubber band is.

3. Put two books on the truck. Pull the truck. Look at how long the rubber band is.

Results:

Describe what happened on your record sheet.

Conclusion:

Which takes more force?
Write your answer on the record sheet.

Moving Light and Heavy Objects

Question:

The push or pull needed to move an object is called force. Which takes more force—moving a light object or a heavy object?

Prediction:

Write what you think is the answer.

_____

_____

_____

_____

_____

Results:

Did the rubber band stretch longer when the truck pulled a light object or a heavy object?

_____

_____

_____

_____

_____

Conclusion:

Which takes more force—moving a light object or a heavy object?

_____

_____

_____

_____

_____

FS-23211 Science Made Simple ▪ © Frank Schaffer Publications, Inc.

DOES FORCE ALWAYS MAKE THINGS MOVE?

Review with the class the fact that a force (such as a push or a pull) is needed to make an object move. Ask the students if they think an object moves every time force is applied to it. Then try this activity.

First, bring out a suitcase filled to capacity. (Make sure the suitcase is heavy enough so that the children will not be able to move it.) Then call on a student volunteer to move the suitcase either by lifting it or dragging it. When the child shows he cannot move the suitcase, ask the class why. Discuss the fact that though the student is exerting force, the suitcase is too heavy for him to move. Tell the class that force does not always make things move.

Next divide the class into small groups and challenge each group to think of a way to move the suitcase. Afterwards, let the groups test their ideas. (Examples: Make the suitcase easier to move by taking out some items; then less force will be needed to move the suitcase. Tie a rope to the suitcase handle and have several children try pulling on the rope together.)

EQUAL FORCES

This simple activity demonstrates the fact that whenever there is a force in one direction, an equal force from the opposite direction can stop things from moving.

First take the children out on a grassy field, pair them up according to size, and have them face their partners. Instruct the students to put their hands on their partners' shoulders. Then tell the children to gently push against their partners. The students will find that neither they nor their partners fall over.

Next have the students stand so that their toes are touching their partners' toes. Then tell the children to hold their partners' wrists and gently lean backward. The students will see that they do not fall over as long as they keep pulling each other with equal force.

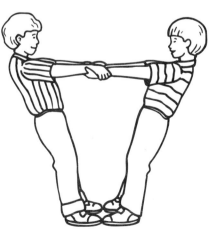

Talk with the class about what happened and ask why none of the students fell over. Explain that when an object is pushed or pulled from one direction, a push or a pull from the opposite direction can stop it from moving.

Simple Machines

Machines are devices that move things. They are designed to help make work easier. Some children may think of machines as complicated equipment with moving parts; however, simple machines, such as a crowbar or an axe, may be made up of only one or two parts. There are six types of simple machines: the lever, the inclined plane, the wedge, the screw, the pulley, and the wheel and axle. As you introduce your students to simple machines, they will see that all machines have the same purpose—to move things when force is applied.

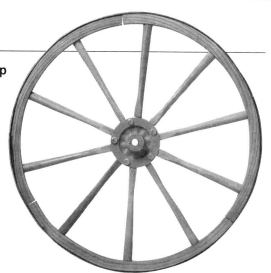

MACHINES HELP US WORK

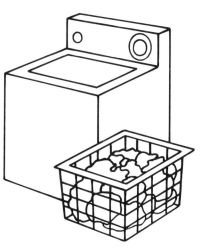

Show your students several articles of clothing and a box of laundry detergent, and ask what they think you might do with the items. (Wash the clothes.) Tell your class you could do the wash by hand, but that there would be a faster way to get the job done. Elicit from the class the fact that a washing machine would allow a person to do the laundry quickly and easily. Next show pictures of other types of machines and discuss their uses (Examples: farming equipment, sewing machine, photocopier, lawn mower) Have the children name other machines and write their suggestions on a sheet of chart paper titled "Machines Help Us Work." Let the students cut out magazine pictures of machines and add them to the chart.

LOOKING AT SIMPLE MACHINES

Show the class a can opener and a pair of scissors. Then show a picture of a washing machine and a lawn mower (or other machines). Ask what the items have in common. (All of them are machines.) Tell the class that machines are tools that help people do work. Explain that machines work by moving things when a force (such as a push) is applied. Tell the students that the can opener and pair of scissors are called *simple machines* because they are not made up of many complicated parts. Then demonstrate how the two items work. Have the students notice the force you have to exert in order to operate the two machines.

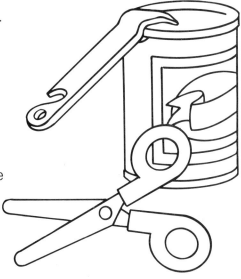

Later create a "Simple Machines Center" in the classroom and let your students examine other simple machines. (See the "Simple Machines Center" activity described on page 35.)

SIMPLE MACHINES CENTER

Learning Center

Display examples of simple machines for your class to examine. Here are some suggestions:

Lever—clothespins, hammer, pliers, nutcracker, scissors

Inclined Plane—cardboard or wooden ramp leading up to the back of a toy truck

Wedge—chisel, plastic knife

Screw—screws, bolts

Pulley—toy crane, drapery rods

Wheel and Axle—toy car with movable wheels, eggbeater, gear wheels in a clock

Discuss how each of the simple machines works. (Examples: A clothespin opens when a person pushes down one end of it. A toy car moves when its wheels turn. A ramp is useful for putting a heavy load into a truck because moving an object up a slope is easier than lifting it upright.)

If you have toy tools, include them at the center for the class to use. Large pieces of plastic foam are ideal for using toy nails and screws. Simply punch holes in the foam ahead of time to make it easier for the students to insert and take out their nails and screws.

WORKING BY HAND AND BY MACHINE

Class Demonstration

This demonstration lets your students compare doing work by hand and by machine.

First, ask two students at a time to do the following (one student per task):

Make whipped cream.

- Beat a bowl of whipped cream with a spoon by hand.

- Beat a bowl of whipped cream with an eggbeater.

Pick up small pieces of paper from the floor.

- Pick up the paper by hand.

- Pick up the paper using a broom and a dustpan.

Crack a nut.

- Crack the nut by hand.

- Crack the nut with a nutcracker. (An adult may need to use the nutcracker.)

Discuss which method was easier for each task and why.

MAKE A LEVER

A lever is used to lift heavy loads. It is made up of a bar that rests on a support (the fulcrum). A person pushes down one end of the bar to lift a load at the other end. Let your class make a lever to find out how this simple machine works.

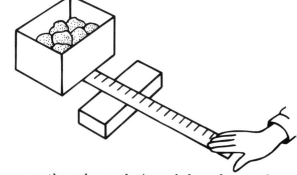

First, tell each child to rest a ruler on a wooden block. Instruct the students to place a weight such as a book, a stapler, or a small box of rocks on the end of the ruler that is closest to the block. Then have each child press down the other end of the ruler. Your students will discover that they can lift the object quite easily.

Have your students vary the position of the block and push down on the ruler each time. Ask such questions as *Did you lift the weight each time? Is it easier to lift the object when the block is in the middle of the ruler or nearer one end?* Your students will discover that the load is easiest to lift when the block is positioned near one end of the ruler close to the object and the pushing point is far away.

LEVERS AT WORK

Bring the following items to school: a shovel, a hammer, a board with a nail hammered into it, a heavy box, and a crowbar. Use the items to demonstrate levers at work.

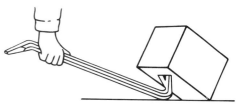

- Take your class outside to show how a shovel is used to dig up dirt. Have a child place the shovel in the ground, push on the handle, and bring up some dirt.

- Demonstrate how the prongs of the hammer can be used to pull out the nail from the board. Point out that pulling on the hammer's handle supplies the force to take out the nail.

- Put a heavy box on the floor. Show how the box can be lifted by placing one end of the crowbar under the box and pushing on the other end.

PLAY A LEVER GAME

Divide the class into small groups and have each group make a lever with a ruler and a small block. (See the activity "Make a Lever" above.) Have the students put their levers on the floor. Next give each group a 12" x 18" sheet of paper and a rolled-up sock. Instruct the children to place the papers a few inches

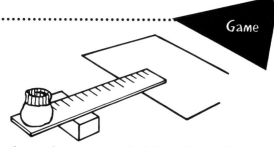

away from their levers. Then have each child take a turn putting the sock on one end of the ruler and pushing down on the other end to hurl the sock through the air. The child scores a point if his or her sock lands on the paper. Let the groups see how many points they can collect in a given time period.

SLIDING AND ROLLING THINGS

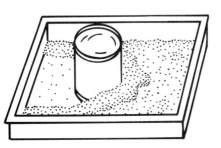

Let your class experiment to find out if it is easier to slide or roll a heavy load across the ground.

First, divide the class into pairs and give each pair a copy of *Sliding and Rolling* (pages 38 and 39). Also provide each pair with two cans and two pans (or shallow boxes) of sand. After your students compare the actions of pushing and rolling the cans across the sand, have them discuss the results. (Your class will discover that it is easier to roll a heavy load rather than slide it along the ground; this is because rolling produces less friction.)

USING ROLLERS

This simple activity demonstrates that objects can be moved by placing rollers underneath them.

Have each student push a book across his desk. Then have the student place three or four straws underneath the book and push again. Ask the class if it is easier to push the book or roll it along. (It is easier to roll the book.)

Tell the students that the wheel is one way people roll things along. Explain that the wheel was invented thousands of years ago, but that no one knows how it was invented. Tell the class that some people think it may have been invented by someone who used logs as rollers to move things.

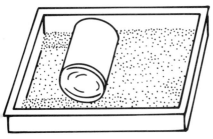

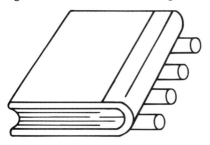

Art Project

All Kinds of Wheels

Divide your class into small groups and have each group make a collage showing different things that use wheels. (Examples: car, truck, roller skates, bicycle, wheelchair, lawn mower, pizza cutter) Students may draw pictures or cut them out from magazines. Invite the children to bring toys that have wheels. Display them on a table in the room for your students to examine.

Sliding and Rolling

Question:

Is it easier to slide or roll a heavy load along the ground?

Prediction:

Write what you think on the record sheet.

Materials:

two pans of sand
two cans

Directions:

1. Put a can in a pan of sand. Stand the can on its end. Push it across the pan.

2. Put a can in another pan of sand. Put the can on its side. Roll the can along.

Results:

Describe what happened on your record sheet.

Conclusion:

Is it easier to slide or roll a heavy load along? Write your answer on the record sheet.

FS-23211 Science Made Simple • © Frank Schaffer Publications, Inc.

Sliding and Rolling

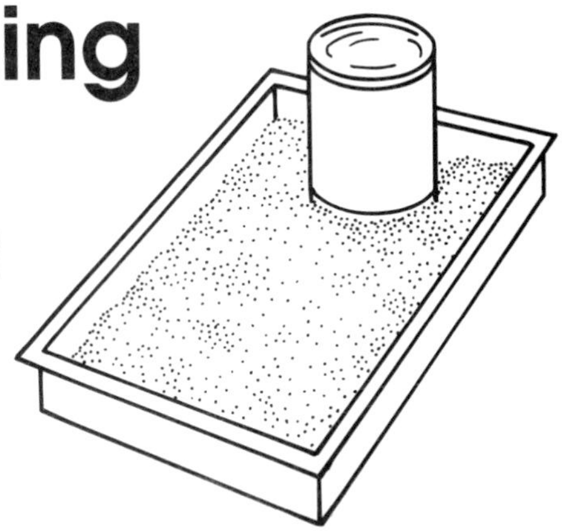

Question:

Is it easier to slide or roll a heavy load along the ground?

Prediction:

Write what you think is the answer.

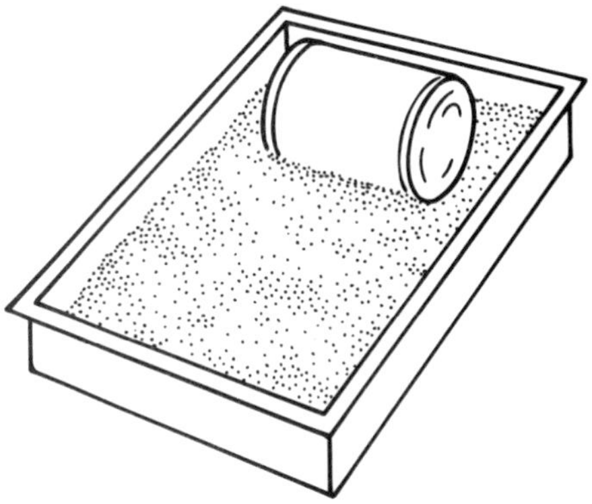

_____

_____

_____

_____

Results:

Was it easier to push or roll the can across the sand?

_____

_____

_____

_____

_____

Conclusion:

Is it easier to slide or roll a heavy load along the ground?

_____

_____

_____

_____

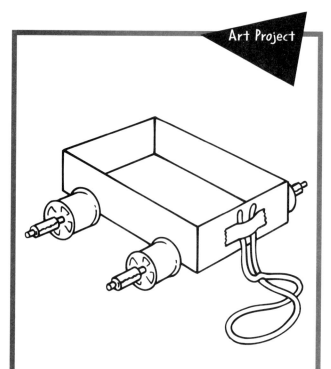

Art Project

Make a Toy With Wheels

Your students will enjoy making a wagon for pulling things. Each child needs four spools (all the same size), two straws, a small box (such as a box for holding checks), yarn, and masking tape.

Give each student a copy of *A Toy With Wheels* (page 41) and have the class follow the directions for making the wagon. If you wish, have the students decorate their wagons by drawing designs with felt markers or gluing on pieces of colored paper.

USING A RAMP *Class Activity*

Ask your students if they have seen people moving things onto the back of a truck using a ramp for sliding things upward. Tell your class that a ramp (an inclined plane) is often used to move heavy loads. Then do this demonstration to show why.

Stack several books on the floor to make a tower about 8 inches high. Rest one end of a board on the books to make a ramp. Next ask a student to lift a heavy book off the floor. Then ask the child to place the book at the bottom of the ramp and move it up the board. The student will find it easier to move the book up the ramp than lifting it. Tell the class that ramps are often used for moving things because it takes less effort to slide a heavy load up or down a slope rather than carrying it up or down directly.

Afterwards, have your students make their own ramps with boards and toy blocks. Let the children practice moving their toy wagons (see "Make a Toy With Wheels" above) and other objects up and down their ramps.

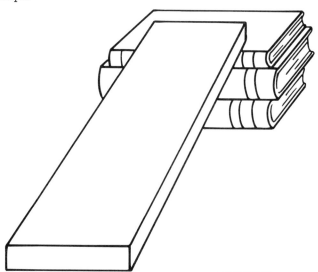

RAMPS HELP PEOPLE *Class Activity*

Tell your class that a person may not think of a ramp as a machine because it looks so simple. Add that ramps are used in many places to help move things. (Examples: A ramp at a supermarket helps people move their grocery carts from the store to their cars; a ramp at a hospital lets people in wheelchairs move into and out of the building easily.) If your school has a ramp, take your class out to see it.

Later, challenge your students to be on the lookout for ramps in their neighborhood. After several days, make a chart listing the different places your students spotted ramps helping people.

A Toy With Wheels

Make a toy with wheels to help you move things.

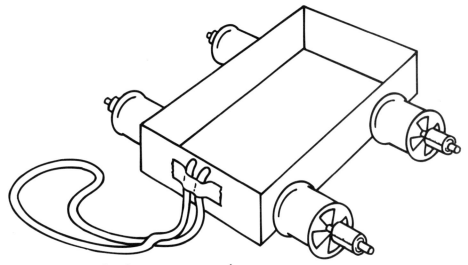

Materials:

four spools
two straws
small box
yarn
masking tape

Directions:

1. Insert each straw through two spools.

2. Wrap some tape around the ends of each straw. This will keep the spools from falling off.

3. Tape the straws to the bottom of a box.

4. Turn the box over. Tape a loop of yarn to one end of the box for a handle.

5. Put something in the box. Have fun pulling your toy along!

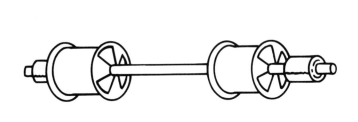

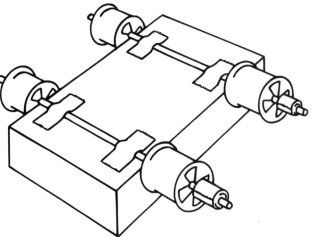

SCREWS GO ROUND AND ROUND

Let your class examine a variety of screws. Have the students notice that the threads wind around the center of the screw's body. Then give each student a turn placing two fingernails at the tip of the screw's thread and turning the head clockwise with the other hand. The students will see that the fingers stay in place but the screw travels downward.

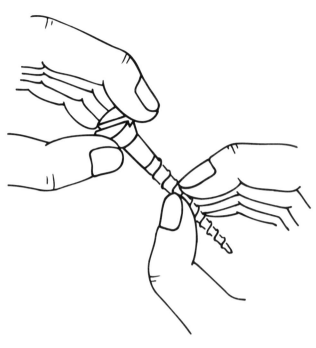

Later, give each student an unsharpened pencil and a copy of *Screws Go Round and Round* (page 43). After the students color the edge of their triangles, instruct them to make the screw according to the directions. The class will see that the colored line "climbs" up the pencil in a winding path. Explain to the students that when a person turns a screw, it moves into or out of an object.

LOOKING FOR SCREWS

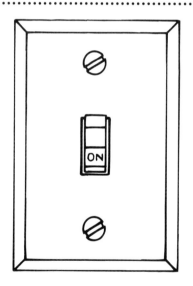

Tell the class that screws are often used to fasten things together. Then give examples by pointing out screws that are used in the classroom. (Example: Screws are used for attaching switchplates to the wall.) For a homework assignment, have the students make a list of the various ways screws are used in their homes. When the children have compiled their lists, ask them to share their findings with the class.

A PULLEY AT SCHOOL

Explain to your class that a pulley is a wheel that holds a rope in place. A person pulls on one end of the rope in order to lift a load attached at the other end. Draperies, for example, are opened and closed using a pulley system. Cranes also use pulleys for lifting loads. Then ask your students if they can think of how a pulley is used at school. After your children share their ideas, take them outside to see the school flag. Point to the rope hanging beside the flagpole and to the wheel located at the top of the pole. Tell your students that pulling on the rope and moving it across the wheel allows a person to raise and lower the flag.

Screws Go Round and Round

The screw is a simple machine.

Make a model of a screw.

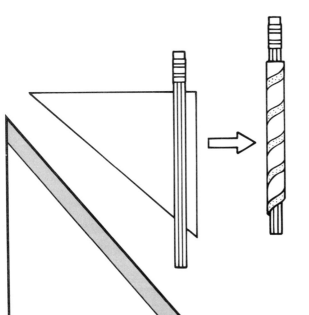

1. Color the shaded edge of the triangle.

2. Cut out the triangle.

3. Lay the paper facedown. Tape the edge to a pencil.

4. Wrap the paper around the pencil. Tape down the end.

Turn over. Tape the pencil here.

Sound

Sounds are everywhere. From birds chirping to machines whirring, sounds surround us throughout the day. Some sounds are quiet while others are very loud; some sounds are unpleasant and annoying while others are melodic and interesting. All sounds, however, have one thing in common—they are produced by the vibrations (rapid back-and-forth movements) of an object.

A LISTENING WALK

Outdoor Activity

Give your students pencils and paper, and take them outdoors on "a listening walk." Every so often, stop for a minute and have the children listen carefully to the sounds around them. Instruct the class to write or draw the source of those sounds. Afterwards, have the children make a class chart listing what they heard on their walk.

WHAT DO I HEAR?

Class Activity

Prepare for this activity by tape-recording 10 different sounds. (Examples: water flowing out of a faucet, a clock ticking, a piano key) Then play the cassette for the class and ask the students to identify the sounds. Have the children describe each sound and explain what clues helped them determine the source.

MAKING DIFFERENT SOUNDS

Group Activity

Divide the class into pairs and give each pair a collection of various materials, such as a sheet of aluminum foil, two metal spoons, a piece of sandpaper, a block of wood, an old toothbrush, a jar, and some buttons. Then have each pair do the following activity.

One student turns his back to his partner. The partner makes a sound with the objects, and the student guesses which materials were used. The two students then switch roles.

Challenge the children to see how many different kinds of sounds they can make with their materials.

WHAT MAKES SOUND?

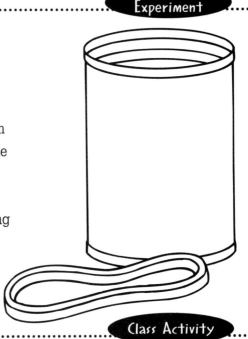

Sound is produced when an object vibrates (moves quickly back and forth). The vibrations of the object cause the surrounding air to vibrate; when the vibrations reach our ears, we hear them as sounds.

Introduce the concept of vibrations to your students by having them do the experiment *What Makes Sound?* (pages 46 and 47). When the students stretch a rubber band across a can and then pluck it, they will hear a sound. Have the children notice how the rubber band moves back and forth when it is plucked. Guide the class into seeing that the vibrations of the rubber band moved the surrounding air and produced sound.

A VIBRATING RULER

This activity reinforces the concept that a vibrating object produces sound. (See the above activity "What Makes Sound?")

Instruct each child to hold a ruler at the edge of a desk with one hand. Then have the students use their other hand to press the end of the ruler down and let go. The class will observe that the ruler vibrates and a sound is produced. Explain that as the ruler moves up and down, it pushes the air around it up and down. Tell the class that these movements are picked up by our ears as sound.

FEELING VIBRATIONS

Have your students put their fingers on their throats and talk or sing. The children will notice that their throats vibrate. Explain that when we we talk or sing, our throats vibrate and produce sound.

Next have your students touch their throats as they sustain a sound, such as a hum or a word ending in a vowel (bee, no, say). They will feel continuous vibrations as long as they keep making the sound. Explain to the class that anything that makes a steady sound vibrates. Tell your students that if they hold their hand against an object that is making a steady sound (such as a refrigerator), they will be able to feel its vibrations. Then give each student a copy of *Feeling Vibrations* (page 48) for a homework assignment. Have each child look for the objects at home and check for vibrations. Afterwards, ask your students to share their findings with the class.

What Makes Sound?

Question:

What happens when you stretch a rubber band across a can and pluck it?

Prediction:

Write what you think on the record sheet.

Materials:

a can
a rubber band

Directions:

1. Stretch a rubber band across the top of the can.

2. Pluck the rubber band.

Results:

Describe what happened on the record sheet.

Conclusion:

Think about the rubber band you plucked.
What do you think makes sound?
Write your answer on the record sheet.

FS-23211 Science Made Simple ▪ © Frank Schaffer Publications, Inc.

What Makes Sound?

Question:
What happens when you stretch a
rubber band across a can and pluck it?

Prediction:
Write what you think is the answer.

_____

- -

_____

_____

- -

_____

Results:
What happened when you plucked the rubber band?

_____

- -

The rubber band **vibrated**. It moved back and forth
quickly. What happened to the air around the rubber
band?

_____

- -

Conclusion:
What do you think makes sound?

_____

- -

_____

_____

- -

_____

FS-23211 Science Made Simple • © Frank Schaffer Publications, Inc.

Feeling Vibrations

Have you heard the refrigerator hum? Have your heard the telephone ring? Objects that make a steady sound are vibrating. They are moving back and forth quickly. If you put your hand against these objects, you can feel the vibrations.

Look for the objects below at home. Hold your hand against them to feel the vibrations. Check off the objects you test.

☐ a refrigerator humming

☐ a computer turned on

☐ a clock ticking

☐ a radio playing loudly

☐ a TV set playing

☐ a washing machine running

What other object makes a steady sound in your home?

_____

_____

Did you feel its vibrations?

_____

_____

FS-23211 *Science Made Simple* ▪ © Frank Schaffer Publications, Inc.

A STRAW FLUTE

Here's a fun activity that demonstrates how the amount of vibrating air affects sound.

Give each student a straw and have him or her gently blow through it. Then tell the class to cut off about one-half inch of the straw and blow again. The students will notice that the sound has changed. Have the children repeat the procedure several times. Discuss the results with the class. (The pitch gets higher as the straw gets shorter.) Ask what caused the change in sound. (the length of the column of air) Explain to the class that the length of the column of air inside the tube affects the kind of sound that is produced. (The longer the column of air, the lower the pitch.)

A SHOEBOX GUITAR

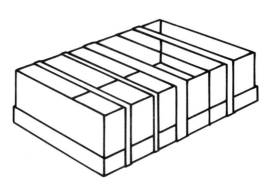

Your class will enjoy making a guitar. First, have each student fit a shoebox inside its lid. (The lid makes the box more sturdy.) Next give every student five rubber bands of varying widths. Instruct the children to wrap the bands around their boxes. Let the students pluck their guitars. Show the class how to change the sound by pulling the sides of the box.

Discuss with the class what vibrates as the guitar is being played. (the rubber bands) Have each child notice the different sounds his or her guitar makes. (Thin bands vibrate more quickly and produce higher sounds while thick rubber bands vibrate more slowly and produce lower sounds. Pulling the sides of the box stretches the bands, resulting in higher sounds.)

MUSICAL GLASSES

Set out five identical drinking glasses and pour different amounts of water into each glass. Ask the class to predict what will happen when you tap each glass with a pencil. (A sound will be made.) Then tap the glasses; your students will notice that each glass makes a different sound. Tell the class that when you tap the glass, the air inside vibrates. The different amounts of air in the glasses result in the different sounds. (The greater the amount of water and the shorter the column of air inside the glass, the higher the sound made.)

Later divide the class into small groups and give each group five drinking glasses. Have each group pour water into the glasses to make a "musical instrument." Then let the students in each group compose a musical piece on their instrument and perform it for the class.

MAKING SOUNDS LOUDER

Gather your class around a radio or tape recorder. Play some music and have your students listen. Then instruct the children to cup their hands around their ears and listen again. The students will discover that the sound becomes louder. Explain that by cupping their hands, they are "collecting sound" and directing it toward their ears.

Next tell the students they will be making paper cones for collecting sounds. Then give each student a 12" x 18" sheet of paper. Show the children how to roll their papers into a cone shape. Have the students tape the edge of the rolled paper down.

Play some music again. Let each child come up to the radio or tape recorder and listen with the narrow end of his cone placed against one ear. The music will seem louder because the cone collects the sound and directs it toward the ear.

SUPER HEARING

Show your class a picture of an African elephant, and have the students notice the animal's ears. Tell your class that the African elephant has the largest ears of any animal. Point out that its outer ears measure about four feet wide and that it can hear sounds made by animals two miles away!

Discuss with your students what it would be like if they woke up one day and discovered they had the hearing ability of an elephant. Ask questions to help the children think about the advantages and disadvantages of having such hearing. (Examples: Would it come in handy if your friends could talk to you from two miles away without having to use the phone? Would it be hard to plan a surprise party for a friend who had super hearing?) Then have each child write a paragraph explaining whether or not he or she would like to have super hearing.

LOUD AND QUIET SOUNDS

Class Activity

Divide a chart into two columns. Label one column *Loud Sounds* and the other *Quiet Sounds.* Then brainstorm with the students things that make loud sounds and things that make quiet sounds. (Examples: *Loud*—cymbals banging, jet plane flying overhead, fire engine siren, train whistle; *Quiet*—baby breathing softly, leaves rustling, a child tiptoeing) Write the students' suggestions on the chart.

Later, have the class make some of the loud and quiet sounds listed on the chart. Here are some suggestions:

- Take the students outdoors and have them make some loud sounds, such as the roaring of a jet plane's engines and the screeching of an ambulance siren.

- Ask the children to show you how quietly they can tiptoe around the room.

- Give each child a sheet of paper. Have the students wave their papers gently in the air to imitate the sound of leaves rustling.

ANNOYING NOISES AND SOOTHING SOUNDS

Group Activity

Read Ann McGovern's *Too Much Noise* (Houghton Mifflin, 1967) to the class. In this delightful tale, an old man named Peter is annoyed by the noises in his home (the bed creaking, the floor squeaking, and so on). The wise man of the village advises Peter to bring various animals into the house one by one. In the end, Peter realizes that the noises which he first thought were loud and distracting are in fact quiet and soothing compared to the noises of the animals.

Afterwards, divide the class into small groups and have each group make a list of unpleasant noises and a list of pleasant sounds. Have the groups compare their lists with one another.

EAR PROTECTORS

Art Project

Discuss people who work in noisy places. (Examples: construction workers, mechanics, factory workers, airport employees) Explain that very loud noise can cause pain and hearing loss. Tell the class that people who work in noisy places must wear special protectors over their ears.

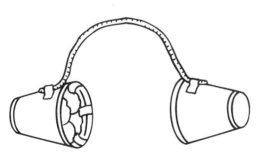

Next let the students make their own ear protectors to show how such equipment works. Give each child two paper cups, some paper towels, a pipe cleaner, tape, and a copy of *Make Ear Protectors* (page 52). Guide the students through the directions.

To test the ear protectors, play a musical selection on a tape recorder. Let your students listen to the music without their ear protectors first and then with their ear protectors on. Have the children compare the sounds. (The students will discover that the ear protectors block out much of the sound.)

Make Ear Protectors

People who work in noisy places must wear special protectors for their ears.

Make some ear protectors for yourself.

Materials:

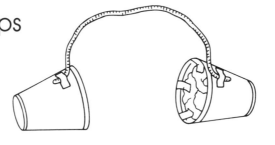

two paper cups
paper towels
pipe cleaner
tape

Directions:

1. Stuff the paper cups with paper towels. Tape the paper towels to the cups so they will not fall out.

2. Tape the ends of the pipe cleaner to the top of the paper cups.

3. Fit the cups over your ears to block out sound.

FS-23211 Science Made Simple ▪ © Frank Schaffer Publications, Inc.

Earth Science

Rocks, clouds, rain, sun—these and other components that make up the environment fill children with curiosity and wonder. *What are rocks made of? What are clouds? Why does it rain? How far away is the sun?* Children eagerly ask questions about what they see around them. As children observe, ponder about, and investigate the objects and materials that make up their world, they gain deeper insights into the nature of the universe.

CONCEPTS

The ideas and activities presented in this section will help children explore the following concepts:

- Rocks and soil are part of the land.
- There are different types of rocks and soil.
- Weather changes from day to day.
- Changes in weather can be observed and measured.
- A shadow forms when an object keeps light from falling on a surface.
- Shadows change in length as the sun moves across the sky.

LITERATURE RESOURCES

These resources will help children learn more about topics related to Earth science.

Weather Words and What They Mean by Gail Gibbons (Holiday House, 1990). Weather terms such as temperature, wind, and moisture are explained in simple terms for children.

Weather Signs by Ann and Jim Merk (Rourke Corporation, 1994). Children learn about signs that help people predict weather: cirrus clouds indicate rain is near, flights of wild geese signal the changing of seasons, and more. Beautiful full-color photos complement the clear, simple text.

Rocks and Minerals by William Russell (Rourke Corporation, 1994). This colorful, easy-to-understand book introduces children to rocks and minerals.

A First Look at Rocks by Millicent E. Selsam and Joyce Hunt (Walker and Co., 1984). The authors teach children to look for distinguishing characteristics that help identify one rock from one another.

My Shadow by Robert Louis Stevenson, illustrated by Ted Rand (Putnam & Grosset Group, 1990). Vibrant watercolor paintings bring Stevenson's delightful poem to life. The artist gives readers a peek at children around the world playing joyfully with their shadows.

Rocks and Soil

Rocks and soil cover much of the Earth's land surface. Rocks are made up of minerals, a nonorganic substance. Soil is composed of minerals as well as plant and animal matter. Rocks vary greatly in color, shape, size, texture, and hardness. Soil varies in color (depending upon its composition) and texture (depending upon the size of the particles that make up the soil). Both rocks and soil are important natural resources.

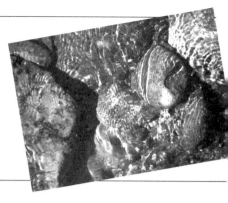

A ROCK COLLECTION

Learning Center

Start a rock collection in your classroom. Ask your students to look for rocks and bring them to school. As the children bring their samples to class, talk about where the rocks were found. Discuss the fact that rocks can be found in many places in the neighborhood.

Next place each rock in a resealable plastic bag. Number the bags and on each one include a label indicating where the rock was found. Later display the rocks at a center where the students can examine them more closely with magnifying glasses. Also provide books that present color photographs of rocks and see if the students can identify any of the rocks in their collection.

A SORTING GAME

Game

Divide the class into small groups and give each group eight or more rocks. Let the students examine the rocks and note qualities such as color, shape, and texture. After the students have had a chance to look at the rocks closely, let them play this game.

First, give every group two pie plates. Then have one student in each group sort the rocks into two categories and place them onto the plates. The other group members examine the rocks and guess what criteria was used to sort the rocks. The game continues with another student in the group sorting the rocks differently.

Here are some characteristics your students may consider in order to determine their groupings: Shiny/Dull; One Color/More Than One Color; Round/Not Round; Smooth/Rough; Big/Little; Sparkly/Not Sparkly; Speckled/Not Speckled; Stripes/No Stripes.

COLOR HUNT

Hold up several rocks and have your class point out the different colors. Discuss the fact that rocks come in a wide variety of colors. Next have each child choose three rocks from your class collection (see "A Rock Collection" on page 54) and tell the students that they will be looking for colors in their rocks. Then give each student a magnifying glass and a copy of *Color Hunt* (page 56). Instruct your students to examine their rocks for the colors listed on their activity sheets.

To allow students to look at individual colors in their rocks more clearly, have them dip their samples in bowls of water. The class will notice that wetting the rocks makes the colors more intense.

Afterwards, discuss the results of the color hunt with the students. Ask the class such questions as *Which color showed up the most? Which color showed up the least? Did any rocks have only one color? Which rock had the greatest number of colors?*

Tell the class that the different colors in each rock indicate the different types of materials (minerals) that make up the rock. (Note: Color by itself is not an accurate clue as to the identity of the mineral because minerals come in different colors.)

TESTING FOR HARDNESS

Let your students test rocks for hardness.

Divide the class into small groups and give each group several rock samples, a penny, and a paper clip. Give every group a copy of *Testing for Hardness* (page 57) and have each student select two rocks to compare. Instruct the students to scratch each rock with a fingernail, a penny, and a paper clip and have them look to see if any marks were left. (To check that the scratches were actually made, have the students wipe the rocks with a damp cloth. The rocks have been scratched if the marks are still there after the rocks have dried.)

After the children try scratching their pairs of rocks, have them test to see which rock is the harder of the two. The rock that leaves a mark on the other is the harder rock.

For a follow-up activity, have each group look at its members' findings and graph how many of their rocks could be scratched by a fingernail, how many by a penny, and how many by a paper clip. Let the groups share their results with one another.

Color Hunt

Look at three different rocks.
Check off the colors you see in each rock.

Rock 1	Rock 2	Rock 3
__ black	__ black	__ black
__ blue	__ blue	__ blue
__ brown	__ brown	__ brown
__ gray	__ gray	__ gray
__ green	__ green	__ green
__ orange	__ orange	__ orange
__ pink	__ pink	__ pink
__ purple	__ purple	__ purple
__ red	__ red	__ red
__ white	__ white	__ white
__ yellow	__ yellow	__ yellow

Testing for Hardness

Get two different rocks. Draw their pictures.

Rock 1

Rock 2

Test the rocks for hardness.

Scratch each rock with a fingernail, a penny, and a paper clip. Were marks left on the rocks? Write **Yes** or **No** on the chart below.

	Fingernail	Penny	Paper Clip
Rock 1			
Rock 2			

Now try scratching each rock with the other.

Which rock left a mark? _____
_____

Which rock is harder? _____
_____

LAYERS OF SOIL

Class Experiment

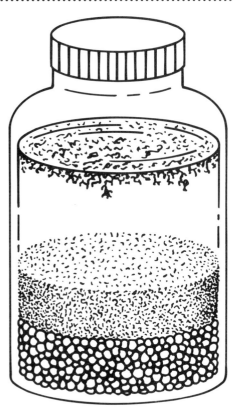

This experiment allows students to separate the different types of materials that make up soil.

First, have each student bring a jar of soil to school. (The jar should be about the size of a mayonnaise bottle.) Then give every child a copy of *Layers of Soil* (pages 59 and 60), and let the class work through the experiment.

After a day, the students will see that their soil has settled into layers at the bottom of the jar with some materials left floating on top of the water. Discuss the fact that soil is made up of different-sized particles. Guide the class into seeing that the largest, heaviest particles settle first, forming the bottom layer. The smallest, lightest particles settle last. Explain that the floating material is called *humus*. Tell the class that humus is made up of dead plants and animals and that it provides nutrients needed for plant growth.

THE IMPORTANCE OF SOIL

Art Project

Show your class pictures that illustrate how plants, animals, and people need soil. (Examples: a farmer working on his land; a field of flowers; animals burrowed into the ground) Tell the class that soil is an important natural resource. Explain that without soil, there would not be any forests or fields, because there would not be any plant life. Animals and people would lose their source of food. Worms, insects, rabbits, moles, and other animals would lose their homes.

Afterwards, get a long sheet of butcher paper and have the class paint a mural showing the different ways soil is used.

FS-23211 Science Made Simple • © Frank Schaffer Publications, Inc.

Layers of Soil

Question:

What happens when you shake a jar of soil and water?

Prediction:

Write what you think on the record sheet.

Materials:

large clear jar with lid
soil
water

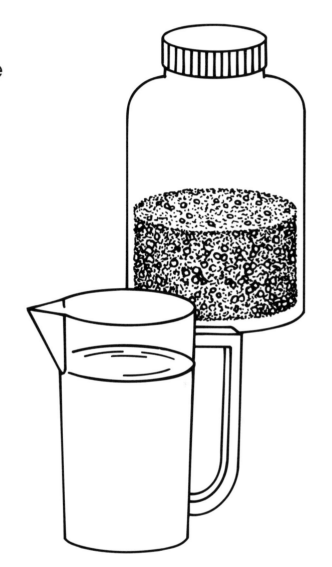

Directions:

1. Fill a jar halfway with soil.

2. Fill the jar to the top with water.

3. Screw on the lid. Shake the jar well.

4. Leave the jar for a day.

Results:

Draw what the soil in the jar looks like.

Conclusion:

Why do you think the soil settled into layers? Write why.

Layers of Soil

Question:

What happens when you shake a jar of soil and water?

Prediction:

What do you think is the answer?

_____

_____

_____

_____

Results:

Draw a picture of what the soil in the jar looks like after a day.

Conclusion:

Why do you think the soil settled into layers?

_____

_____

_____

_____

_____

_____

FS-23211 Science Made Simple ▪ © Frank Schaffer Publications, Inc.

Weather

Weather is an important part of people's lives. It influences what people wear and often affects their choice of activities. Weather is constantly changing. As your students observe and investigate weather, they will discover that changes in weather are related to changes in the atmosphere, the air that surrounds the Earth. They will also see that changes in weather are associated with the changing seasons.

WEATHER IS ALWAYS CHANGING

Class Activity

Hold up the weather report from a newspaper and ask the students to identify it. Then read parts of the report to the students and ask them why people would want to know about the weather. (Examples: People make plans about what to wear and what to do depending on the weather; travelers like to know about weather conditions in the places they are going so they can pack appropriate clothing.) Elicit from the class the fact that weather is an important part of people's daily lives.

Next ask the students to look outside and describe the day's weather. (If it is a pleasant day, you may wish to take the class outdoors for this activity.) Encourage the children to describe what they see (such as the types of clouds or the color of the sky) as well as what they feel (hot, cold, windy, and so on). Ask the children if they think the weather report in the newspaper will be exactly the same for tomorrow. Continue by asking if the present weather conditions will be exactly the same for the weekend. Guide the students into seeing that weather is always changing. Tell the class that because weather can be very different from one day to the next, a service such as weather reporting helps people prepare for weather changes.

WEATHER WORDS

Class Activity

Have the class brainstorm a list of words that describe weather conditions or elements of weather. Write each word on a strip of paper. Then have each student illustrate the meaning of a word. Post the words on a large sheet of paper for a handy reference chart. Here are some words you might include on your chart:

blizzard	fog	lightning	storm
breeze	frost	mist	sunny
cloud	hail	rain	thunder
dew	hurricane	rainbow	tornado
drizzle	icicle	sleet	wind

WHAT WILL I WEAR?

Class Activity

Show your class various articles of clothing that are worn in particular types of weather. (Examples: swimsuit, shorts, sunglasses, mittens, raincoat, scarf, boots) Hold up each item and ask the students what kind of weather it is suitable for. Discuss with the class the fact that people wear clothes that are suitable to the type of weather they are experiencing.

Next give each student a copy of *What Will I Wear?* (page 63). Instruct the children to draw articles of clothing in each box. The pictures should show clothes and accessories that are appropriate for the type of weather described. When the activity sheets are completed, let the children share their drawings with the class.

All Kinds of Weather

Divide the class into groups and have each group make a colorful collage showing various kinds of weather. Let the students glue magazine pictures or drawings onto large sheets of butcher paper. The children may also add paper shapes that they have cut to represent raindrops, clouds, and snowflakes.

WEATHER WATCH

Class Activity

Beginning on a Monday, have the class record the weather for one week to see how much conditions vary during that time.

First, give each student a copy of *Weather Watch* (page 64). Tell the students that they will be drawing one or more symbols each day to show what the weather is like. Have the students record their observations at the same time each day so that the comparisons of weather conditions are more accurate. For Saturday and Sunday, let the children take their record sheets home; or have the students make their observations on a separate sheet of paper and instruct them to copy the weather drawings when they return to school the following week.

After the seven days have been charted, discuss the results with the class. Talk about how the weather changed or stayed the same during the course of the week. Ask the students to predict what the weather will be like the following day, and let them check their guess the next day.

Name_____

What Will I Wear?

Read about each type of weather.
Draw a picture to show what you will wear.

warm and sunny

cool and windy

cool and rainy

cold and snowy

Name _____

Weather Watch

	☼ sunny	☁ cloudy	🌧 rainy	🌬 windy	❄ snowy
Monday					
Tuesday					
Wednesday					
Thursday					
Friday					
Saturday					
Sunday					

Write the number to show how many days were

sunny ____   cloudy ____   rainy ____   windy ____   snowy ____

WHAT WARMS THE EARTH?

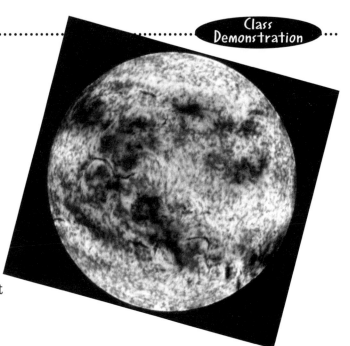

Class Demonstration

This simple demonstration shows that the sun heats the Earth.

On a warm day, have the children hold their hands a few inches from a shaded window that faces the sun. Then lift the shade and have the students hold their hands up to the window again. They will notice that their hands feel warmer. Ask the class where the warmth they feel comes from. (the sun) Explain that even though the sun is millions of miles away, its heat reaches the Earth and warms us. Tell the students that they will be doing various activities that show how the sun's heat affects our weather.

UP AND DOWN THE THERMOMETER

Class Activity

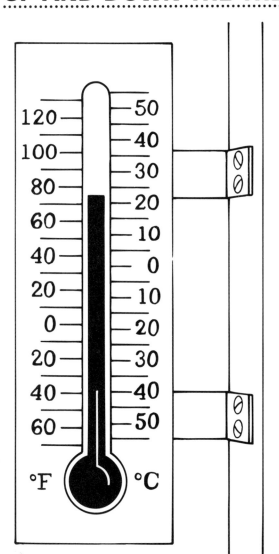

Show your students a thermometer and tell them that the instrument measures air temperature (how warm or cold the air is). Point to the mercury inside the thermometer and explain that the mercury moves up when the air around it is warmed and moves down when the air is cooled. Ask the children how they think the air gets warmed. (by the sun)

Next display the thermometer outdoors where the students can read it easily. (Keep the thermometer out of direct sunlight.) Then measure the temperature every hour, beginning with when the students first arrive at school and ending with a reading near the end of the school day. Record the temperatures on a sheet of chart paper. Repeat the procedure for two or three days.

Your class will observe that the temperature rises during the morning and falls during the afternoon. Guide your class into seeing that as the sun rises, the air gets warmer and as the sun sets, the air gets cooler. Tell the students that the difference in temperature occurs because the sun's rays are hotter the higher the sun is in the sky.

WARMEST AND COLDEST DAYS

Set a thermometer outside in a shady spot and let the class keep track of the temperature for a week. Each day at the same time take the students out to check the thermometer. Record the temperature on a chart. After a week, have the students note which day was the warmest and which one was the coldest.

CLOUD SHAPES

Class Activity

Do this activity on a day when there are clouds in the sky. First, show your class pictures of different types of clouds. (These pictures can be found in encyclopedias and in library books.) Ask the children to describe what they see. Tell the class that there are three main kinds of clouds. Then give each child a copy of *Cloud Shapes* (page 67), and discuss the clouds shown on the page. Explain that clouds are often signs of the type of weather that is coming. For example, large puffy clouds (cumulus) generally mean fair weather while sheetlike clouds (stratus) usually bring rain or snow.

Next take the class outside to look at clouds. Have the children draw a picture of the clouds they see and write what kind of clouds they might be. Let the students share their opinions with the class.

Art Project

Cloud Pictures

Give each child a sheet of blue paper and some cotton balls. Then have the students first draw scenes and afterwards glue on clouds made from cotton balls. Show the class how to gently pull apart the cotton balls to make various shapes. When the pictures are completed, display them in the classroom and have the students guess what type of clouds each child made.

Cloud Shapes

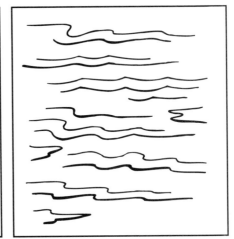

Clouds have different shapes.
There are three main kinds of clouds.

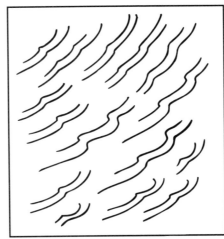

Cumulus clouds are fluffy.

Cirrus clouds are thin and high.

Stratus clouds look like layers.

Go outside.
Look at the sky.
Draw the
clouds you see.

What kind of clouds do you think they are?

WARMING THE LAND AND WATER

Tell your class that when the sun heats the Earth, it warms both the land and the water. Ask your students, *Which do you think gets hotter faster—land or water?* Then have the class do the experiment titled *Land and Water* (pages 69 and 70). The experiment may be done as a class demonstration or as a small group activity.

In the experiment your class will discover that the soil and the water begin at the same temperature but that the soil warms up more quickly. At the end of an hour, the temperature of the soil is higher than that of the water.

Discuss the results of the experiment with the class. Tell the students that when the sun heats the Earth, some parts get warmer than others. Explain that this uneven heating of the Earth is one reason why different areas have different temperatures.

WIND IS MOVING AIR

Art Project

Make a paper fan and wave it back and forth near your students. Ask what they feel. (a wind) Tell your students that wind is moving air. The children felt a wind because you were moving the air with a fan.

Inform your class that movements in hot and cold air produce winds that affect the weather. Explain that the Earth and the air surrounding it are heated by the sun. Because all parts of the Earth are not heated evenly (see the activity "Warming the Land and Water" above), the air that lies over the warmer areas are warmer than the air that lies over the cooler areas. Tell the class that warm air rises. Explain that when this happens, the cooler air rushes in to take its place; this movement of air results in wind.

For a fun follow-up activity, let the students make their own paper fans for moving the air and "creating" wind.

Land and Water

Question:

Which heats faster—land or water?

Prediction:

Write what you think on the record sheet.

Materials:

two plastic cups
two thermometers
soil
water
paper towel

Directions:

1. Fill one cup half full of water.
   Fill the other half full of soil.

2. Set the cups in a sunny spot.
   Put a thermometer in each.

3. Take the temperatures after one minute.

4. Take the temperatures after a half-hour and after an hour.

Results:

Write the temperatures on the record sheet.

Conclusion:

Which heats faster—land or water? Write what you found out on the record sheet.

Land and Water

Question:

Which heats faster—land or water?

Prediction:

What do you think is the answer?

_____

- -

_____

Results:

	Temperature after a minute	Temperature after half an hour	Temperature after an hour
Soil			
Water			

Conclusions:

Which heats up faster—land or water?

_____

- -

_____

Suppose it were a sunny day. Would it be warmer on land or in the ocean?

_____

- -

_____

FS-23211 Science Made Simple ▪ © Frank Schaffer Publications, Inc.

WEATHER AND SEASONS

Ask the students what season they are in right now. Then have the class name the various weather conditions that are characteristic of that season. For example, is it cool, warm, cold, or hot? Is there much rain, fog, or snow? (Your students' answers will reflect the type of region you live in.)

Ask the class to name the other seasons and to describe the type of weather associated with each one. Guide the students into seeing that the weather changes as the seasons change. Add that in most places temperatures are the hottest during the summer months and coldest during the winter.

Next tell your students to pretend that a pen pal is planning to visit their area. Have each student think about which season would be the best time for visiting in terms of the kind of weather the area will be experiencing. Ask each student to write a letter telling which season he would recommend for travel and why. Let the students share their letters with one another.

MY FAVORITE WEATHER

Ask the students to tell which is their favorite season and why. After the children give their responses, let them make booklets about their favorite weather.

First, provide each child with a copy of *My Favorite Weather* (page 72) and instruct the class to complete the sentences. Then have the students cut out the sentence strips.

Next give each student four sheets of drawing paper. Instruct the students to glue a sentence strip onto each sheet and to draw a picture illustrating the sentence. Then staple the pages together along with construction paper covers. Have the students share their work with one another.

My Favorite Weather

Make a book about your favorite weather.
Complete each sentence.
Cut out the sentence strips.
Glue each strip onto a sheet of paper.
Draw a picture. Staple the pages together.

The kind of weather I like best is

_____

- -

_____

During my favorite kind of weather I like to wear

_____

- -

_____

One thing I enjoy doing in this kind of weather is

_____

- -

_____

In this kind of weather I enjoy eating

_____

- -

_____

FS-23211 Science Made Simple ▪ © Frank Schaffer Publications, Inc.

Shadows

Shadows are formed when an object blocks the path of light. The object prevents the light from shining on a surface, and it casts a darkness where the light would have fallen. On a sunny day, a person blocks the path of sunlight and casts a shadow that is in the shape of his or her body. As your students experiment with shadows, they will discover that there are certain factors which influence a shadow's appearance.

WHERE DO SHADOWS FALL?

Class Activity

Place a filmstrip projector on a table or desk several feet from the wall. Shine the projector's light onto the wall. Then have the students stand in front of the projector. (Tell the children not to look directly at the bright light since it can hurt their eyes.) Ask the children where their shadows fall. (They fall behind them.) Ask if there is any way to make the shadows fall in front of them. (The children can turn their backs to the light.) Point out that no matter how the students position themselves, their shadows fall from the side of them that is opposite to the light source. If the students face the light, their shadows fall from their back side; if the students' backs are to the light; their shadows fall from their front side.

MY SHADOW TWIN

Art Project

Tape a large sheet of black construction paper to the wall and shine a projector's light on it. Have a student stand in front of the projector. Ask the class to describe the student's shadow. (The shadow is in the shape of the student's body.) Have the student turn and face different directions. Ask the other students if they can identify the person simply by looking at his or her shadow.

Next call on one student at a time to stand in front of the light so that his or her silhouette falls on the paper. Trace each child's shadow (head, neck, and shoulders) onto the paper using chalk. Instruct the students to cut out their silhouettes and glue them onto white paper. Display the silhouettes around the room and see if the students can identify the person in each picture.

WHAT'S MAKING THE SHADOW?

Here's a fun guessing game that sharpens children's observation skills. You will need a filmstrip projector (or other source of light) and several objects with distinguishing shapes (such as a fork, a pair of scissors, a pencil, a mug, a key, and a paper clip).

Put a filmstrip projector on a table or desk and have it face the wall. Place the table or desk in the room so that the class can sit between the projector and the wall.

Have the students face the wall. Darken the room and then shine the projector's light against the wall. Hold up one object at a time in front of the projector so that its shadow is cast in front of the children. Have the students try to identify the object by its shadow.

SHADOW PICTURES WITH HANDS

Class Activity

Let your students use their hands to make shadow pictures of animals. Shine a projector's light on the wall and let one or more children at a time hold up their hands to the light. Encourage your class to try making ducks, rabbits, dogs, and other animals.

MAKING SHADOWS CHANGE

Group Activity

In this activity students discover they can change a shadow's appearance by moving an object closer to or farther away from the light source. They also see that shadows are affected by the angle at which the light hits the object

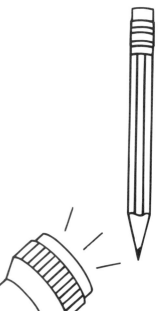

First, divide the class into pairs and give each pair a flashlight, a pencil, and a copy of *Making Shadows Change* (page 75). Then have the students follow the directions on the activity sheet. During the activity, one partner holds the pencil straight up and down while the other student shines the flashlight on it. The class will discover the following:

1. Moving the pencil toward the flashlight makes the shadow bigger.

2. Moving the pencil away from the flashlight makes the shadow smaller.

3. The shadow is darker and clearer when the pencil is closer to the wall.

4. When the flashlight shines on the pencil from the side, the shadow becomes more fuzzy.

FS-23211 Science Made Simple ▪ © Frank Schaffer Publications, Inc.

Making Shadows Change

Work with a partner. One person will hold a pencil against the wall. The other will shine a light on the pencil.

1. Move the pencil toward the flashlight. Does the shadow get bigger or smaller?

_____

- -

_____

2. Move the pencil away from the flashlight. Does the shadow get bigger or smaller?

_____

- -

_____

3. Make the shadow as dark and clear as possible. Is the pencil closer to the flashlight or to the wall?

_____

- -

_____

4. Point the flashlight directly behind the pencil and the wall. They will be in a straight line. Move the light so that it hits the pencil from the side. What happens to the shadow?

_____

- -

_____

LOOKING FOR SHADOWS

Take the students outside on a sunny day and have them look for shadows. Tell the children to be on the lookout for shadows with interesting shapes. (Examples: leafy plants, spider webs, railings) When a shadow is sighted, have the class look to see what object is blocking the light to cause the shadow. Also have the students describe the shadow's appearance. To help sharpen their observation skills, ask such questions as *How can you tell what is making the shadow? Do you see long, straight lines or wavy lines? Are some parts of the shadow darker or lighter than other parts?*

Later discuss the shadows with the children and ask them to name the shadows they thought were especially interesting or beautiful. Then give each child a copy of *Looking for Shadows* (page 77) for a homework assignment. Tell the students they may look for shadows either indoors or outdoors. Encourage the children to look for shadows that have interesting features such as repeating lines, unusual shapes, or beautiful patterns.

HOW LONG IS MY SHADOW?

This activity demonstrates the fact that the sun's position in the sky affects the length of shadows.

Divide the class into pairs and give each pair a measuring tape, a piece of chalk, and a copy of *How Long Is My Shadow?* (page 78). Then take the students outside onto a flat, paved area. Give each pair the following instructions:

1. One partner stands with the sun shining on his or her back so that the shadow falls in front of the child. The other partner uses the chalk to trace around the shadow.

2. Measure the shadow from head to toe. Record the length on the activity sheet. Also record the time. (Young children may find it easier to do this activity on the hour or half-hour.)

3. Repeat the activity an hour later, standing at the same spot. Label your shadows. Do the activity again two more times after that. (Four measurements will be taken.)

Your students will discover that their shadows change in length. They will also see that the shadows change position. Shadows are the shortest when the sun is high in the sky (noon). Shadows are the longest when the sun is lower in the sky (when it is rising or setting). In the morning, the sun rises in the east and shadows fall westward. In the afternoon, the sun begins setting in the west and shadows fall eastward.

FS-23211 Science Made Simple • © Frank Schaffer Publications, Inc

Looking for Shadows

Look for different kinds of shadows.
Fill in the chart below.

Shadow	What Made the Shadow	What the Shadow Looked Like
a big shadow		
a little shadow		
a shadow with an unusual shape		
a beautiful shadow		
a shadow with interesting lines or patterns		

FS-23211 Science Made Simple ▪ © Frank Schaffer Publications, Inc.

Student A _____

Student B _____

How Long Is My Shadow?

Stand with your back to the sun.
Have a partner trace your shadow
with chalk. Measure your shadow.

Repeat the activity one, two, and
three hours later.

Time of Day	Length of Shadow

1. When was your shadow the longest? _____

2. When was your shadow the shortest? _____

3. Was your shadow in the same place each time? _____

FS-23211 Science Made Simple ▪ © Frank Schaffer Publications, Inc.